A CABIN FULL OF MICE

by Janet Foster

A book by OWL
Published in Canada by Greey de Pencier Books, 1980,
Published simultaneously in the United States in 1992 by Firefly
(U.S.) Inc., P.O. Box 1338, Ellicott Station, Buffalo, NY 14205
© 1980 Janet Foster
ISBN 0-919872-66-2
Printed in Canada
OWL is a Trademark of the Young Naturalist Foundation

I knew the very first night that we were going to be sharing our cabin. Soon after dark, when all was still, strange little noises came from the kitchen. There was a gentle "clink," a muffled thump, then a soft scraping sound as though something was being pulled across the floor.

I tiptoed through the cabin and peered around the kitchen door. I could see the snowshoes standing in the corner and the winter firewood piled by the stove. Everything seemed to be in order. Had I imagined those strange noises? Then something rustled in the woodpile. There, gazing up at me, was a tiny creature with the brightest pair of black eyes I had ever seen.

Soon I discovered that our little visitor was not alone. An entire family of deermice was moving in for the winter. The mystery was solved.

Each night the mice appeared, their cheeks bulging with sunflower seeds stolen from the birdfeeder outside. They found tiny openings between the logs and scampered in on secret trails, up the wall and into the roof. Somewhere up there in the soft insulation material they were building their nest.

During the day there was no sign of the mice, but as soon as darkness fell they glided about like little grey ghosts. They climbed the kitchen curtain, swung on the light cord, raced over the countertops and disappeared into the drawers. No shelf was too high for them to reach and no opening too small for them to squeeze through.

Peanuts left out at night vanished by morning. Cookie boxes had small holes neatly scissored out by sharp teeth. Paper towels were shredded into long streamers that mysteriously disappeared. But that wasn't all the little thieves stole. One night, in the darkness, I could see a small shadow pulling out long strands of bright wool from the bedspread. Wherever their nest was, it was going to be warm!

Soon I came to recognize the mice that shared our cabin. One was a deeper grey than the others, another was more brown. Some were adventurous and bold, others were shy. But the most curious—and the most mischievous of all—was Misca. We played games with her, and no matter where we hid the peanuts she loved so much, she was sure to find them.

One night I left a thick wad of cotton wool in the middle of the bedroom dresser. On her way down from the nest, Misca stopped and stared at this mountain of whiteness blocking her path. Cautiously, she reached out and touched it, feeling the softness. Then, quick as a flash, she gathered the billowy bundle between her paws. Looking like a miniature Santa Claus, she climbed back up to the nest.

Outside the cabin the mice were busy gathering fallen seeds from the birdfeeder and carrying them back to store inside the roof. Sometimes from the window I could see Misca scurrying over the snowdrifts like a blown leaf. Then suddenly she would disappear into a network of trails the mice had tunnelled through the snow.

I watched as other wild night creatures moved about in the dark. A snowshoe rabbit, almost invisible against the snow, hopped silently among the trees. A flying squirrel glided from nowhere to land with a gentle "plop" on the birdfeeder. A raccoon shuffled up the snowy path to the cabin and noisily climbed onto the window tray. His sharp nose told him there was juicy fat hanging there. One swipe with a paw . . . then another . . . and down it came.

All through the winter the mice led full and contented lives. With their warm nest safely tucked away in the roof, and a plentiful supply of food inside and outside the cabin, living was easy. They grew bolder and bolder. One night, Misca and a small grey mouse slipped out of the cabin as usual. As they cleaned up the fallen birdseed like little vacuum cleaners, they forgot that sometimes danger waits in the darkness . . .

Up in the old maple beyond the gate, a shadow moved. Floating on silent wings, a saw-whet owl glided through the air and landed in a small birch beside the cabin. The snow was deep, food had been scarce, and the owl was very hungry. He hunted by sound, and the faint scuffling of the two little mice in the snow told the owl exactly where they were.

Stuffing one last seed into her already bulging cheeks, Misca turned and headed back to the cabin. Not a moment too soon! Without a sound, the owl swooped down onto the little grey mouse still under the birdfeeder. Grasping its small body between powerful claws, the night hunter flew back to the woods as silently as it had come.

Owls must eat too, and at least for one cold winter night, this one would not be hungry.

Winter slowly passed and spring came again, as it always comes, with a rush of warmth and new life. There was new life inside the cabin too. Our mice had been giving birth to large families in the roof.

Soon the babies were following their parents across the roof rafters, down the walls and along familiar trails through the cabin. They were growing fast. Before long we couldn't tell which ones were the adults. Sadly, we knew it was time to move them all back to the woods—their natural home. There were too many mice for one small cabin. But how could we catch them?

Remembering their love for peanuts and their amazing sense of smell, we balanced a wooden ruler laden with peanut butter over a large empty pail. Moments later, there was a rustling sound and Misca appeared on top of the woodpile, her nose twitching. Jumping onto the "gangplank," she ran toward the peanut butter, overbalanced the ruler and fell into the pail. There she was, surrounded by walls on all sides that were too smooth to climb and too high to jump.

Was Misca frightened? Not one bit! She calmly settled down and nibbled the sunflower seeds we had sprinkled in the pail. When I put my hand in, she reached up and sniffed my fingers. And then, quick as a wink, she was up my arm, across the shoulder, down my back and away. I scarcely felt her go. "Probably enjoyed the adventure," I whispered as we reset the ruler.

By morning, we had caught ten deermice... or was it eleven? And sitting right in the middle was Misca, who by now must have thought we were playing a new game.

This time, I dangled a long string invitingly above her. Grasping it between tiny silken paws, Misca climbed up faster than a sailor on a rope and stood in the palm of my hand. "I know where I am," she seemed to be saying. But we knew it was time to say goodbye.

Carrying Misca and all the other mice in the pail, we walked down the lane, through the woods and across three fields to a stonepile a long way from the cabin. There we released them. One disappeared into a hole halfway up a tree trunk, another buried himself under a mound of leaves, still another headed into the grassy field.

Just for a moment Misca looked back at us, then she vanished into the stonepile. I felt sad to see the mice go. But I knew they would soon be laying down new trails and building new nests in the wild where they belonged.

Two nights later as we sat before the fire, the cabin seemed strangely empty. All through the winter the mice had given us hours of enjoyment and we were missing them. Then, just as we stood up to turn out the lights for bed, I heard a soft scraping sound coming from the ceiling. I looked up and a familiar furry face peeked out at me over the rafter. Misca was back!

Canadian Cataloguing in Publication Data

Foster, Janet, 1940-
    A cabin full of mice

(Owl's true-life adventure series)

ISBN 0-919872-66-2

1. Mice—Juvenile literature. I. Title. II. Series.

QL795.M37F67   j599.32'33   C80-094584-0

Photographs by John and Janet Foster

```
599.32    Foster, Janet, 1940-
FOS       A cabin full of
C.2       mice / by Janet
          Foster
```